T0097143

The Great Whirl of Exile

poems by
Leroy V. Quintana

curbstone press

FIRST EDITION, 1999
Copyright © 1999 by Leroy Quintana
All Rights Reserved

Printed on acid-free paper by Best Book/Transcontinental Printing

Cover design: East Side Graphics

Printed in Canada

This book was published with the support of the
Connecticut Commission on the Arts and donations
from many individuals. We are very grateful for this
support.

Library of Congress Cataloging-in-Publication Data

Quintana, Leroy.
The great whirl of exile : poems / by Leroy V. Quintana. —1st
ed.
    p.   cm.
  ISBN 1-880684-60-8
  1. Mexican Americans—Poetry.   I. Title.
PS3567.U365G7   1999b
811'.54—dc21   99-17698

published by
CURBSTONE PRESS   321 Jackson Street   Willimantic, CT 06226
        phone: (860) 423-5110   e-mail: info@curbstone.org
                http://www.curbstone.org

Table of Contents

II. DEDICATIONS

III. OMEN

It's well known that he who returns never left,
so I traced and retraced my life,
changing clothes and planets,
So I traced and retraced my life,
growing used to company,
to the great whirl of exile,
to the great solitude of bells tolling.

—Pablo Neruda
Fully Empowered

PREFACE

The Great Whirl of Exile is a comforting book in that it is
spread through with an actual life, a living place, animated
by the breathing eyes of a poet.

The poet begins from the top of the light, by quoting
Neruda, to place himself among the number of the
dangerously conscious. So that even with the quietness and
matter-of-factness with which Quintana surrounds his
talking eyes, it adds up. Image, tone, irony, understatement,
emergency seen as something that went down, tragedy as
one riveting color in the spectrum, the voice easy to listen
to, but not quite next to us. That is what we want to know:
where is this voice coming from?

But the book's title, to evoke Neruda, one of the great
poets of the world (like so many of them, speaking
Spanish...Guillen, Cardenal, Castillo, Dalton, Vallejo,
Lorca...) suggests what it is to be speaking as an "American"
from the exile of this society's missing humanity and
distanced from the emotional and psychologically
perceived "centers" of a self-determining historic Spanish-
Latino linguistic culture.

Yet there is in the calm exterior of the poetry the stable
persona who describes so precisely his world, confirmation
that Quintana's community/isle is connected to all the
living parts of the American whole. Wherein, as rhythm,
the eyes beat blood into the brain as it rationalizes feeling

xi

into thought. And we get a steady flow of observations, decisions, cautionary tales, commitments, judgments, acceptances and dismissals that fill in another part of our selves and our society that is rarely penetrated with the depth of the actual. Humanity, in all its pain and twisting frustration, struggling to emerge, to return from exile, finally, to some place where Human Beings can live and consciousness is no longer dangerous.

Amiri Baraka 3/99

The Great Whirl of Exile

I

LEGENDS OF HOME

Legends of Home

I

Saturday night turns into Sunday morning turns
into a story drenched in flames. Listen:

They were teenagers trapped inside themselves
searching for freedom the only way youth knows.

You can still hear the car flying off the road
into a telephone pole, the cable snapping,
the flames' thirst for the spilled gasoline.

II

Saturday night spins into Sunday morning spins
into a story of Russian Roulette and how,
when the final turn came, Louie put the gun
to his head and said I guess I lose.

I Go Live with My Mother after Being Raised by My Grandparents

*"To begin to speak of things you find
hard to confess."—George Seferis*

She's at the far end, anxious, uncertain, by the sink.
I pause to look at the four or five small fish,
a streak of iridescent blue running
down their sides as they swim, lurch
in the bowl on top of the table in the middle
of the kitchen, fish she's brought especially
for this occasion. I pretend to be captivated.
I've embarrassed her in front of my aunt
who's driven the 244 miles to bring me home.
I can't pretend I'm happy to be here.

Forty years later, I realize I have been waiting,
waiting my entire life for some one
to take those first steps toward me, simply
because I have been worth waiting for.

Oh mother,
there is an ocean between us.

Tonsils

I am certain, though I'm terrified of doctors and numbers
that I can count back from a hundred all the way to one,
and keep my tonsils, but when I awaken I am unable
to remember if the ether overtook me at ninety-five or
ninety-one.

I get up to face the same unsuspecting day one more time.
Going home is far easier than the dutiful bus
we took to downtown, and from there to north Fourth,
the opposite edge of the city: a quick cab yellow as
the pudding, a row of Vanilla Wafers, like hungry suns
setting in a creamy saffron sea encircling the brim
of the glittering bowl Doña Cruzita, my mother's widowed
                                                    friend
has brought to sweeten the sharp, tight-fisted pain of
                                                swallowing.

Though she does not say so, I have been brave
in the only way my mother knows how to define it.

Mail Order

I've received the dumbbells and the special exercise guide
I sent away for, with only a passing worry about money.

Shortly after that, a letter arrives, stating
that at two p.m. next Wednesday, a lawyer,
with the sheriff at his side, will be at my door.

An eighth grader, I've never been so scared. This is worse,
far worse, than getting my ass kicked by the old pachucos.
But my mother rescues me, had it figured out all along.
A lesson that served me well, at least until my interest
in Astronomy, which ended when she dragged me downtown
to Kilroy's to cancel my beautiful Past Due telescope
I thought I could afford on that great layaway plan.

Faithfully as Well as Exactly

It was about 1958 or so when we finally got a phone,
but the only girl I had enough nerve to call
was the one who seemed to whisper, faithfully
as well as exactly, what time it was, any time I called.

Friday Night

Friday night was for parrandas. Time, now, that the daily grind
has worked itself to a stop, for a good time, a good time;
to live beyond the day-to-day measure of time and worth;
to live while the tired world sleeps its weary sleep.

Next door, that no good (as far as my mother is concerned)
step-uncle whacking away on his helpless twelve string,
drunker and drunker on Schlitz, wailing at the darkening moon,
along with his pachuco in-laws long past the News, Sgt. Bilko,
The Honeymooners, farther, deeper into the night,
as Lon Chaney grappled between man and wolf on Horror
                                                    Theater.

Sunday Afternoons

Her hair is the color of fire enjoying itself;
roots dark as the Headless Horseman's heart.

All I have to do to do what Tony is doing
which is kissing her girlfriend
the way both Ichabod and Brom dream
of ravishing the schoolmistress
is reach over the seat, she's unafraid, waiting,

and, and, she's mine, as easy as the rest
of the girls seem to be for Tony,
who, before long, gets his girlfriend pregnant
at seventeen and vanishes from Sleepy Hollow
forever.

Leonard

Suddenly he was in American History that summer,
old enough to smoke the crooked L&M's
he carried in his always rumpled white shirt.
Hair parted in a zig zag; thick glasses
sitting awkwardly on his nose; always in need of a shave.
He dragged his left leg, undaunted, day after day.
Home was Oklahoma; that much he revealed.
Who knew where he lived? We had an idea of how.

Soon he had us interested in gun magazines.
One day, after class, we followed him downtown,
Tuttle's Used Goods, where he knew where to find
that mag with photos of a naked man holding a shaving mug,
his genitals sweetly covered with sudsy cream.

Could it be true a woman had put a gun
to his head, forced his face between her legs?

The Girls from Peralta, New Mexico

The girls from Peralta were, oh, so snooty,
and for no reason. They were not as beautiful
as they believed themselves to be, certainly not
as smart; they refused to speak Spanish,
but their English was laughable; for example,
they claimed their houses were Espic and Espan,
because that's what they used, and recommended.

So it seemed only fitting that people mocked them
by breaking the name of their town in two,
translating "Per" into "Pear," and "alta" into high,
and naming them forever "Las High Pears."

What It Was Like

If you want to know what
it was like, I'll tell you
what my tío told me.
There was a truck driver,
Antonio, who could handle a
rig as easily in reverse as
anybody else straight ahead.

Too bad he's a Mexican was
what my tío said the
Anglos had to say
about that.

And thus the moral:

Where do you begin if
you begin with if
you're too good
it's too bad?

Zen—Where I'm From

You simply have to admire how, immediately after
the twelve-foot high chain link fence
crowned with coils of wicked barbed wire was
erected, the fence the City Council voted on
unanimously to guard against anyone ever again,
again breaking into one of the town's
storage sheds, how immediately after, the
thieves drove up with their welding torches and
stole it!

Packing Peaches

He owned a small orchard next to the road
that led to my mother's childhood home, and
whenever anyone passing by greeted him, asked
how he was, he is remembered only and always
for replying "Oh, packing peaches, packing peaches"
which everybody presumed meant
he was doing fine, just fine.

The New Underpass

The town council has given us a new underpass.
Now we don't have to take the long way to town.
Soon the smell of urine is so strong
you have to hold your breath, or put a Kleenex
over your mouth and nose as grandma does.
The lights suffer from blackeyes and the walls wear
the initials of the pachucos, their wicked loves,
like wretched tattoos.
                              To be delivered
into the light of day, the lucky side of tracks,
you have to step carefully, step, cautiously, step
around the children of timeworn and humble coalminers.

Duck Lady—El Paso

A woman, a fat woman
with a big ass,
is walking,
a bucket in one hand.

Furthermore,
she is heading
towards the pen,
a bucket swinging
from the other hand.

Also,
the long white
blouse she is wearing
rises, then falls
over her ass
just like a duck's tail.

And,
most importantly,
there is a duck
behind her,
waddling just like she does.
And behind
the duck,
a string of ducklings.

Drunk In English

Whenever don Andres got drunk with an Anglo
he'd tie the reins to the saddle horn,
let his old horse lead himself home,
and, slowly rocking in the saddle,
nod to everybody along the way,
mutter he was borracho en Inglés.

Pepe

By the beginning of school the following day
he was a legend, to be known forever
as the one who scrambled madly down
the street, both hands desperately
holding his guts from splattering,
sliced neatly in a sensational rumble
that otherwise would have been nothing
more than a morning's worth of cool gossip.

Tires So Thin You Could See the Air
& a Wedding Ring Cheap as a Lugnut

Filemón says he was so poor
when he was first married
he was driving around on tires
so thin que se podia ver el aire.

As for Senaida, she can look back now and laugh,
as if amazed her wedding ring was so cheap,
and, oh, so dreadfully plain, no other way for her
to describe it than to call it her wedding tuerca.

The Locksmith Goes Fishing

I have spent my life returning people's lives to them.
It's a good thing I'm an honest man.
The entire world presumes I carry the answer
to every closed door.
My wife's life and mine are secured against thieves.
Her heart the only lock whose secret I never spilled.
The doors of my life have no keyholes.

With the Lights On All Night

In English, to say that somebody slept with the lights on
all night can be trusted to mean nothing else, but so much
is lost in Spanish when you say that Alfredo slept all night
con la luz prendida unless you know that his wife's name
is Luz which means light, and that prendida can mean the light
was left on, or that Luz was clinging to him, toda la noche,
madly.

The Corner of the Fish Market on Broadway and Coal

Filemón says he had a hand in constructing
our culture, directly responsible for
some of the architecture. You see,
he was an ambulance driver and one time
he was going so fast, oh, ochenta maybe,
two wheels, turned and demolished the
corner of the Fish Market on Broadway
and Coal, the east end of the viaduct.

It's true. Drive by there, he says, and
you'll see how they didn't even bother
to build it back up at a right angle.

187

In California there are one hundred and eighty-seven reasons
for a beating. Everything about you is illegal except your hands.
May they move fast, move fast, then move on.
Pray for rain.

Poem for U-Haul

The highway was made for a morning like this.
A woman with two sad blackeyes. Never
again, never, never again. Last night
was the last time, the last time, the last.

Working at the Tribune

It's Love! oh, Love! And the world must know!
The world must know that it's Love! Love! Love!

It's Love! It's Love! at seventy three Love!
Love again! Love, love again! Oh, again Love!

He's brought her, his love, along with their picture,
for the world, the world to know, his second wife.

Oh Love oh Love! for the second time! Eternal
love years after the death of his first wife.

Oh Love! Oh Love! can compel a man, Love!
to paste the pictures of a new love, crazy Love, oh!

of the new wife over the face of the old,
and for the new love, Oh foolish Love! not to mind.

Those People Who Drink a Lot of Wine

One day Lalo happened by drunker than usual,
and in the middle of a sentence forgot the name
of those people who drink a lot of wine.

No, it wasn't the Italianos, and no it wasn't
los Franceses; the name of those people,
he demanded, impatiently, who drink a lot of wine!
No, goddamnit, it wasn't the Greeks!

Who was left? We sat, silent, stunned and intimidated
as fools with their first big paycheck.

¡Winos! ¡Winos! he exclaimed suddenly. That was the name
of those people who drink a lot of wine! Then added,
we had to be pretty damned stupid
not to know something as simple as that.

Etymology: Chicano

Filemon says that when the movimiento began,
a talkshow host attempted to clarify
how the word "Chicano" originated.

A woman called in, assuredly said
it had its roots in "chicanery,"

those people being such liars and thieves,
so dishonest and deceitful.

Nicknames

The talk turned to nicknames the other day
and Filemon said the man who worked next
to him in the mine and burst into song
all day long was called Caruso,
and the guy who admired his sandwich
and smacked all through the lunch hour,
that was El Sabroso, and the one burned
pretty bad in the smelter, why he
came to be known as El Chicharrón.

Grammar

Filemon says he was talking to Juan, an old friend of his,
who went to college, and eventually became a professor.
And so Filemon asked him "Oye, tu que estas tan educado,
tell me, which is correct?" he wanted to know
once and forever which is proper "pos" or "pues."
His friend thought about it a while
and then matter-of-factly said "Pos, pues."

The Rockets' Red Glare

The Super Bowl had come to San Diego; the rich
rub elbows with Bob Hope.
We get fireworks.

The woman behind me asks her son
how so many rockets can be set off in succession.

You just hire a bunch of Mexicans to run around
with a lot of matches.

Isn't it great, she sighs, bombs bursting in air,
to be an American?

II

DEDICATIONS

Poem for Josephine Baker

It flew in through the kitchen window
that summer a few years after the war,
the year I turned four or five,
that fragile yellow bird Made In Japan
whose insides had been sucked out
when the bomb fell on Hiroshima.

All it required for nourishment
was the sweet, cold water
I poured into the slot in its back.

When I blew on the tail feathers,
experimenting with trills, warbling
like some lonely sax man
'round midnight in his sleepless room,
an exile in graceful Paris,
I didn't know then, in that small town,
the other side of the tracks,
I had learned a little, enough
of the sweet language of the birds.

When that song fluttered into my life again
I knew how to say "Hello. Welcome!" and
"My. It's been a long, long time."

Poem for Fats Domino

Friday night and there's a dance in the cafeteria.
There is a God, perhaps the one the nuns use to keep in line.

I've put on my shirt, tie and jacket, ready, willing and able
to rock 'n roll all night long, as long as it's a waltz.

But my stepfather says I'm not going at all if I'm going like that:
wearing a $10 jacket with a $2 pair of pants. He doesn't care

about cool; doesn't say much when it comes to rules
so I take off the khakis and slide on some dress pants.

First thing Freddy says is I was supposed to dress cool,
he's ashamed to be seen with me. All my learning is going to
                                                          come

this hard. We stroll up Broadway singing "Blueberry Hill,"
and when we get to school I stand by the punch bowl,

the record player, venture out every fourth or fifth song
'cause I can't, just can't learn the first part of the jitterbug,

the part before you start twirling a girl, whirling, cool,
so I waltz with the girl who is as well mannered

as I am coarse, who is my age, and soon
her body will be raging with cancer.

Poem for Myron Floren

What could be more boring than shuffling
into the gym to listen to some square
from Lawrence Welk's band play the accordion
just because his niece, who's got to be a big square
herself, convinced the principal, no cost to the school?

But he never gave us a chance to doubt him.
Yeah, he was a square squeezing some old-
fashioned tunes out of an instrument as popular
as acne, but we quickly learned to say hip
in his language: it didn't matter what you did,
it was how much you loved it that counted,
as well as doing it in front of the disbelievers
shamelessly, but not like the Marine Corps
recruiting sergeant, who also charmed us when
his turn came around the end of our senior year.

Poem for Harry Houdini

What a delight that summer, page after page,
slipping out of hicktown jails, out of trunks
strapped tight and dropped into the ocean,
sliding out of miles of chains twined around
you like serpents squeezing your last sigh from you.

I have slipped through the fingers of my grandparents' home
forever, taken away to live with my mother and stepfather.

Your nimble fingers allow you to unbuckle
straitjackets, squirm to freedom.

You go from town to town, leaving
the dictionaries humbled, wailing,
the definition of escape
continuously evading them.

Poem for Uncle Rudy

What Uncle Rudy hates most is the thought
of turning a dollar bill loose, of allowing
a penny a breath of fresh air. Nickels
and dimes grow so sick and tired of each
other living in his pockets for decades.

So it's not surprising he came up
with his own cure for back pain
instead of going to see the chiropractor.

He had one of his sons hang him from his feet,
like a shark down on his luck, but the rope
slipped and Uncle Rudy landed on his head.

He got up smiling, however, dusted himself
off, said he was feeling better already.

Poem for Marilyn Monroe

Proof is what mathematicians' wives contend with.
The more proof you require the better the whiskey.

Therefore, if there is a storm, or say
your minimum wage pays for three weeks and a couple of days
out of the month and electricity turns its back on you,
you need only pull three socks out of five
from your dresser drawer to find a match.

The owner agrees; he posed the question,
but no matter what brand of truth you offer,
the chap next in line for the best fish and chips
in Albuquerque, or New Mexico, in other words, the world,
is harder to convince than an enraged tax collector.

It's an easy world; all that needs to be done to be considered
an adult is to lift that plastic sheet over that picture
of hers on the calendar, and her clothes come off. Easy.
Nobody has to worry about what thirteen-year-olds
have to say or what miracles they pray for.

Poem for Rod Serling

You make a wrong turn one day;
you think you know why.
It's the same town, nothing's
changed though you were last
here eighteen years ago, the same
town you were raised in,
the same town even though you're lost.

You've seen the great cities of the world,
but never these groomed avenues, two-story
houses; you've stepped into
one of the Currier and Ives prints
that came inside those fabulous boxes
of Raisin Bran you collected long ago
when you lived in that green house
by the unpaved road, on the opposite
edge of the universe.

Poem for Toby Lee

Today, water is not worth all the blood
that has been spilled over it.

Fish have learned to weep.

The Rio Grande swallows its tears.

Mermaids look to the heavens and proclaim "Fraud!"

A new law should be enacted: a lifetime must
last longer than eighteen months.

I drink from her lips,
her first lover.

The ambulance arrives; the driver wraps her
in *The Las Cruces Sun-News.*

Poem for Pancho Gonzales

This was the world of white lines, a game
unlike any other, where the object was to win,
only you used words like "Please"
if your aim ended up improperly
in the next court, "Thank you" when
the ball was returned and "Love"
after you scored first.

Yours was the name that survived
the hatred only California can inspire,
strong enough to be etched in fire
on tennis rackets redeemed
by thrifty mothers who built a life
on S&H Green Stamps a dish,
a dish, a lamp, an ashtray at a time.

Poem for Grandpa

Grandpa had a furious temper; when angered
cursed fiercely. Even though he knew
only a few words of English
started out by taking the Lord's name in vain
which was followed by what was clearly Spanish,
and then with what would have been fluent English
had he been born in Brooklyn and not New Mexico.

Poem for Joey Limas

I was there the night you battled
Gaspar Ortega, your fists as fast
as his, whirling defiant counter punches;
you beat the champ, at worst a draw.
But the money wasn't on you.

I, who had not learned to hit back,
never stopped being proud of you.
Even though you were quiet, a gentleman,
your fists were ungracious.

This was not the first time you lost
in your own home town.
This had always been,
and would forever be, Palookaville.

Poem for Salt

The biggest snowstorm to hit Denver in twenty years.
What is the world to do, freed from the shackles
of the eight hours needed to earn its daily salary?

Only on a day such as this does salt overshadow gold.
Salt, with its lips of blue fire, common as gossip,
ordinary as sin. Like true love and gasoline,
missed only when they run out. Salt spilling
from a blue container a young girl is holding,
along with an umbrella, on the label of a blue
container of salt that the woman across the street,
under her umbrella is pouring behind her left rear wheel,
to no avail this discontented, unbuttoned December morning.

Poem for Pavlov

My primo got tired of people breaking
into his house so he bought a Doberman,
named him Ezra, which, if you like
poetry, could make for a vicious watchdog,
mean as a divorce lawyer with a hangover,
or, if you prefer whiskey, could mean
a dog smooth as a reformed catholic
peddling insurance door to door
to the common and illiterate.

But my primo underestimated the people
in the hood who understood the evils
and benefits of science: he kept finding silent,
merciless rocks dreaming idly in his yard,
and it wasn't until they broke in again,
took everything they didn't take previously,
that he realized that poor mutt had been stoned
every single time his neighbors walked by,
until he was gracious as a fainthearted innkeeper.

Poem for a Vietnamese Student

Some words have tongues sharp as punji stakes.
They lie awake in ambush as long as necessary,
sometimes in the shadows of other words: gobbledygook.

They know the future because they have no regret
for the past. They are ill-mannered, pretend to be deaf
as clocks, in love with the sound of their names.
They lie awake in ambush as long as necessary,
sometimes in the shadow of other words: gobbledygook.

They find their way into our blood, and haunt us.
We pay with our lives all our lives.

Welcome to America. Sin loi. Get your dictionary,
go to the board, look up a new word: write down
guide words, entry word, phonetic spelling, learn
how to pronounce the word, which syllable is stressed.
Repeat after me: gobbledygook, gobbledygook, gobbledygook.

III

OMEN

Omen

*(A Poem For My Daughter Sandra
On Her Twenty-fifth Birthday)*

Suddenly our laws are suspended.
The neighborhood wino maneuvers
his way home comfortably
because it is the world that is stumbling.

The hospital sways like a stripper
who knows how to take things slowly.

Logic has fled the country
like a thieving dictator loaded down
with the tax dollars he promised
would unburden the poor.

At the very moment gravity is held
at gunpoint Horror Theater begins
with another rerun of the earth trembling,
splitting open, the evil that has hidden
underneath for so long now ready
to take its rightful place among us.

The old woman who shares the waiting-
room with me, no longer sure
if lead sinks, if North is still where it was,
asks me in Spanish to decipher
which catastrophe was real, which illusion

This is how your life begins.

At the New Mexico
Viet Nam Veterans' Memorial

The doctors failed to banish Viet Nam forever
when they removed the tumors from his brain.

Jagged centipedes crawl out of his dreams, and tread
down his forehead, nearly tumbling into his blue eyes.

Unlike the devil who went back to hell after the war,
home for him is now a village somewhere in Mexico.

The curse of a country that endeavored
to paint the jungle a resplendent orange.

Before a Year in Viet Nam

We crossed the bridge into South Carolina
simply to get the hell out of Georgia,
and especially out of Ft. Gordon
for the simple magic of frothy beer.
An ordinary Saturday night in the south
so the bartender refused to serve Sammy.
The simple magic of a frothy beer.
Simply because we were young and soldiers.

Gook Nigger

Hard luck means being born in Viet Nam,
and turning thirteen in the middle of a war.

As if that were not enough, life
is complicated by the hazards of blackness,
the hardships of having been born a woman.

We are here to save your country from Communism.
Hard Luck. Blessed are the peacemakers with their M-16's.

That Country

That summer was the summer my naughty hands
unchained themselves eagerly from my wrists,
and, recklessly indulgent, touched
your younger sister's girlish breasts.
She didn't tell, and I thought then
that would be all there was
of a story that was also about you.

We had prayed the entire school year
for peace, and for the fall of communism,
as we had the year before, and would
the year after that, and the year after that.

The world was primarily us, then Russia,
along with Fatima, and wherever in Mexico
the Virgin had miraculously appeared; the Vatican;
of course, there was Cincinnati, that splendid city
back east where the mother-house was,
and, unforeseen, a country in southwest Indochina,
completely disregarded in Geography,
that country that would someday claim your legs.

Lesson

Years later, I remember staring at your thrift store highheels,
long out of fashion, much too formal for everyday wear.

A suit at least half a size too big; no amount of pride
would ever be enough to tailor it to your taste.

Up until then the worst law was the one that stated if
a friend flunked, or got pregnant, you never saw him or her
                                                        again,

and/or if you did it was worse, far worse than
what any dictionary would ever have to say about shame.

Portrait

A woman waits for the 8:15 to Georgia, is waiting.
It could be 7 p.m., a possessive, haunting Saturday
in Fayetteville, North Carolina, as the evening is drowning
in the gasping wheat field of night, evening spinning
into darkness black as she is black, she knows
the answers to the great and volatile questions of her life
so she wears an elegant cobalt-blue suit, matching
incredulous high-heeled shoes, a blasphemous pillbox hat,
dabs on some rouge, the right shade, I suppose
of lipstick, red as her radiant nails, then runs
a chaste, open-hearted comb through her mustache,
those two outstretched wings of a perfect blackbird.

Sharks

When men purchase suits made from our skin
they become dukes, barons of giant corporations
with thousands of loyal employees producing
mirrors, locks, bibles, perfumes and
phosphorescent matches, all vital
for the survival of their countries.

Soup made from our fins makes men
want to slurp their way
up and down womens' calves.

Our jaws can provoke nightmares
a thousand miles inland, when displayed
dangling over the silver spoons, cameos
and other precious heirlooms
locked in glass cases, along
with the stale copies of Life
sleeping in the corners of antique shoppes
anywhere there is a Main Street.

Only gangs that are cool name themselves
after us, bold red letters
dripping blood down the backs
of their smooth black leather jackets.

We swim towards blood the way
some people cross an imaginary line
into the United States to pick lettuce,
or sink their hands into small oceans

of soapy water, bring dishes back to life
iridescent as oyster shells slurped dry
at a Republican fund-raiser for the governor
of California who will later pour gas
into the ocean and hand out match sticks.

Like the lettuce pickers and dishwashers,
all we are good for is fighting, trouble.
We carry fearsome switchblades, and
are born knowing how to use them.

Poem for Our Dog
Afraid of Thunder on a Rainy Day

I know what it is like to be so afraid
on a rain-soaked day such as this.
On a rain-soaked day such as this
in Viet Nam I prayed fervently.
In Viet Nam I prayed fervently
shivering uncontrollably in the mud.
Shivering uncontrollably in the mud
as men whose duty it was to kill me filed by
As men whose duty it was to kill me filed by
only a little more than a yard away
Only a little more than a yard away
on a rain-soaked day such as this.
The type of day that dogs don't understand.

Freedom

Some time ago, back home, a man escaped. Vanished.
From the state penitentiary up in Santa Fe.
Suddenly gone like heels on a pair of cheap shoes
you thought would last long past February.

Made his way down to Albuquerque, city of suspicious
and bleeding tempers.
Where he sliced his way through the smoke.
The tired gossip. And held up a bar.

Took all the trampled money that had been waiting.
Faithful as a wild sweetheart. For him baby. Only him.
Leaving the hardened regulars with something real
to talk about. Bitter witnesses of a practical brand of magic.

By the time it took the most experienced of the patrons
to down half a dozen glasses of stagnant beer he was back.
This time in such a saucy blue-black suit proper for weddings,
funerals. A night out to celebrate. Run up a tab on a good
                                                    whiskey.

His shipwrecked face fresh, oddly recognizable
in the buried guilt of the numbed mirror.
He had forgotten how much he had envied that part
of himself that had never been shackled to himself.

About the Author

For those who know his history, it is no surprise that Leroy V. Quintana is a great storyteller in his poetry. He was raised in Albuquerque by Mexican grandparents, who told him numerous folk-tales (*Cuentos*) as a child. "In many ways, I'm still basically a small-town New Mexico boy carrying on the oral tradition," he comments.

Quintana served in Vietnam in the Army Airborne and a Long Range Reconnaissance Patrol unit in 1967-68. His poetry and fiction have appeared in numerous journals and anthologies. Two of his poetry collections, *Sangre* and *The History of Home,* won the Before Columbus Foundation's American Book Award. He has also received a Border Regional Library Association Award. His other books include *Hijo de Pueblo: New Mexico Poems, Interrogations,* and *My Hair Turning Gray Among Strangers.* Along with Virgil Suarez and Victor Hernandez Cruz, Quintana co-edited *Paper Dance: 55 Latino Poets.*

Quintana has taught literature at several colleges and universities, and is currently on the English faculty at Mesa College, San Diego.

CURBSTONE PRESS, INC.

is a non-profit publishing house dedicated to literature that reflects a commitment to social change, with an emphasis on contemporary writing from Latino, Latin American and Vietnamese cultures. Curbstone presents writers who give voice to the unheard in a language that goes beyond denunciation to celebrate, honor and teach. Curbstone builds bridges between its writers and the public – from inner-city to rural areas, colleges to community centers, children to adults. Curbstone seeks out the highest aesthetic expression of the dedication to human rights and intercultural understanding: poetry, testimonies, novels, stories, and children's books.

This mission requires more than just producing books. It requires ensuring that as many people as possible know about these books and read them. To achieve this, a large portion of Curbstone's schedule is dedicated to arranging tours and programs for its authors, working with public school and university teachers to enrich curricula, reaching out to underserved audiences by donating books and conducting readings and community programs, and promoting discussion in the media. It is only through these combined efforts that literature can truly make a difference.

Curbstone Press, like all non-profit presses, depends on the support of individuals, foundations, and government agencies to bring you, the reader, works of literary merit and social significance which might not find a place in profit-driven publishing channels, and to bring the authors and their books into communities across the country. Our sincere thanks to the many individuals who support this endeavor and to the following businesses, foundations and government agencies: Adaptec, Josef and Anni Albers Foundation, Connecticut Commission on the Arts, Connecticut Arts Endowment Fund, Connecticut Humanities Council, Lannan Foundation, Lawson Valentine Foundation, National Endowment for the Arts, Open Society Institute, Puffin Foundation, and the Edward C. & Ann T. Roberts Foundation.

Please support Curbstone's efforts to present the diverse voices and views that make our culture richer. Tax-deductible donations can be made by check or credit card to:
Curbstone Press, 321 Jackson Street, Willimantic, CT 06226
phone: (860) 423-5110   fax: (860) 423-9242
www.curbstone.org